You Mean
So Much
to Me

I'll give this to you,
just to let you know
how much I want you
how much I need you
and how very much
I love you.

Other books by

Blue Mountain Press INC.

Come Into the Mountains, Dear Friend
by Susan Polis Schutz
I Want to Laugh, I Want to Cry
by Susan Polis Schutz
Peace Flows from the Sky
by Susan Polis Schutz
Someone Else to Love
by Susan Polis Schutz
I'm Not That Kind of Girl
by Susan Polis Schutz
Yours If You Ask
by Susan Polis Schutz
Love, Live and Share
by Susan Polis Schutz
Find Happiness In Everything You Do
by Susan Polis Schutz

The Language of Friendship
The Language of Love
The Language of Happiness
The Desiderata of Happiness
by Max Ehrmann
I Care About Your Happiness
by Kahlil Gibran/Mary Haskell
I Wish You Good Spaces
Gordon Lightfoot
We Are All Children Searching for Love
by Leonard Nimoy
Come Be with Me
by Leonard Nimoy
Creeds to Love and Live By
On the Wings of Friendship
You've Got a Friend
Carole King
With You There and Me Here
The Dawn of Friendship
Once Only
by jonivan
You and Me Against the World
Paul Williams
Reach Out for Your Dreams
I Promise You My Love
Thank You for Being My Parents
A Mother's Love
A Friend Forever
gentle freedom, gentle courage
diane westlake
You Are Always My Friend
When We Are Apart
It's Nice to Know Someone Like You
by Peter McWilliams
These Words Are for You
by Leonard Nimoy
It Isn't Always Easy
My Sister, My Friend
Thoughts of Love
Thoughts of You, My Friend
Love Isn't Always Easy
Don't Ever Give Up Your Dreams

You Mean So Much to Me

A collection of poems on love
Edited by Susan Polis Schutz

Blue Mountain Press ™

Library of Congress Number: 82-74103
ISBN: 0-88396-184-9

Manufactured in the United States of America
First Printing: January, 1983
Second Printing: August, 1983

The following works have previously appeared in Blue Mountain Arts publications:

"You mean so much to me," by Jamie Delere and "There are so many things," by Andrew Tawney. Copyright ©Blue Mountain Arts, Inc., 1981. "When things are confused," "Let me be the person," and "I am always here," by Susan Polis Schutz. Copyright ©Stephen Schutz and Susan Polis Schutz, 1982. "It's fun to get a little sentimental," by Laine Parsons; "You may think that I haven't noticed," by amanda pierce; "Please . . . listen closely," by Andrew Tawney; "Love is . . . ," by Beth Lee; "You, Wonderful You," by Laine Parsons; "Let's never stop," by amanda pierce; and "There will never be . . . ," by Laine Parsons. Copyright ©Blue Mountain Arts, Inc., 1983. All rights reserved.

Thanks to the Blue Mountain Arts creative staff.

ACKNOWLEDGMENTS appear on page 62.

Blue Mountain Press INC.

P.O. Box 4549, Boulder, Colorado 80306

CONTENTS

You mean so much to me —
   and I just wanted
   you to know
   how very much I care . . .
You mean so much to me —
   you've helped me to find
   a special outlook on life
   that was hiding
   deep inside of me,
   waiting just for someone like you
   to open the door
   and set it free
You mean so much to me —
   for you've been there,
   through the good times and the bad,
   drying the tears and
   holding back the loneliness —
   giving me a friendly shoulder
   to lean on
   and enough smiles to last a lifetime
You mean so much to me —
   and I can't help but feel
   as though I owe you so much more
   than I can ever repay. . .

But if there's a way —
any way
to hold and to help,
to provide and to encourage,
to give even a part of what
you have blessed me with,
I will be there for you
And wherever time will take us . . .
wherever we may be,
I always want you
    to remember
how much
you mean to me.

— Jamie Delere

If I could give you
one thing,
I would give you
the ability to see
yourself
as others see you . . .
then you would realize
what a truly special
person
you are.

— Barbara A. Billings

When things are confused
I discuss them with you
until they make sense

When something good happens
you are the first person I tell
so I can share my happiness

When I don't know what to do in a situation
I ask your opinion
and weigh it heavily with mine

When I am lonely
I call you
because I never feel alone with you . . .

When I have a problem
I ask for your help
because your wiseness helps me to solve it

When I want to have fun
I want to be with you
because we have such a great time together

When I want to talk to someone
I always talk to you
because you understand me

When I want the truth about something
I call you
because you are so honest

It is so essential
to have you in my life
Thank you for being my friend
Thank you for being my love

— Susan Polis Schutz

I have given a lot of thought
to the impact that our love has
    on our lives
It feels so good to care for you
in such a unique and special way
But should the offer of myself
    ever become a burden to you,
all you need to do is tell me
    and I will back away
though it will surely be the
    hardest thing ever in my life
I know that what I must give you,
    above all else, is freedom —
the right to come and go,
        to be yourself
no matter where that path
        may lead . . .

Even though what I give to you
   is not perfect,
it is offered in the purest
   and most honest way that
     I know how
I hope you will stay in my life
   and share with me
     for a long, long while.

— Johnnie Rosenauer

i wish for you warmth
when it is cold outside

i wish for you a star
when the night is dark

i wish for you courage
when the world is afraid

i think of you, i wish for you
and i hope you know —
that here, there is a heart
and a home;
and here, there is someone
who loves you
more than any wish could
            ever give.

— laura west

Did you know . . . That there is no one in my world besides you with whom I can spend an entire day doing whatever comes along with never a thought for anyone else — feeling completely satisfied because we are together?

Did you know . . . That there is no one besides you whom I can talk to openly and honestly knowing our love will only grow and feeling a need for nothing but our conversation?

Did you know . . . That there is no one more comfortable for me than you — whom I can enjoy silence with and never have a need to fill the space between us because there is no space? . . .

Did you know . . . That no one has ever
made me as happy as you have or loved me
so completely — Never have I known true
intimacy until we grew to where we are?

Did you know . . . That in loving you, I
have experienced feelings far beyond
any I could have imagined and far better
than any I believed possible?

— Genevieve Bartels Wichmann

Once
when I was younger
I climbed to the top
of a large mountain
and it was
magnificent
I felt as though
I was on top
of the earth
and everything
looked so beautiful
and full of life
as if my eyes
had just been opened
to a new world
It was a magic
I cannot adequately
describe, but
it is similar
to the way I feel
with you.

— Rowland R. Hoskins, Jr.

Our relationship
has taught me more
than any book
ever could.
It has given me
the courage to be
honest with my thoughts,
giving all I have to give
and never holding back.
My sense of pride
and my feelings of confidence
are stronger now
than they've ever
been before.

Through you,
wonderful you,
I have discovered
a little more of myself.

— Marci Dee Lowinger

It's fun to get
a little sentimental
   every now and then, my love . . .
thinking back, remembering
   so many nice days
   that you were such a
      special part of;
days that I recall with a smile,
times that I remember with a sigh.

Let's always continue on, you and I,
   doing the things that give us
precious todays
and memories that will add
   so much
      to our tomorrows.

— Laine Parsons

The thing that counts most
in the pursuit of happiness
is choosing
the right traveling companion.

— Adrian Anderson

One who walks
a road with love
will never
walk the road
alone.

— C. T. Davis

Constant companion
light of my days and nights
you are loyalty and love
asking nothing . . . giving all
my heart is full
for you have filled it

— diane westlake

Let me be the person
that you walk with in the mountains
Let me be the person
that you pick flowers with
Let me be the person
that you tell all your inner feelings to
Let me be the person
that you talk to in confidence
Let me be the person
that you turn to in sadness
Let me be the person
that you smile with in happiness
Let me be the person
that you
love

— Susan Polis Schutz

As each day goes by
I find that
I am moving into new depths and
   new dimensions;
I am discovering new feelings and
   new emotions.
Each day is different
and carries with it
its own unique aspect of beauty.
And with each new day,
I find myself falling
   deeper and deeper in love
                with you.

— Colleen Williams

If at times you think
that I take you for granted,
know that it is only
because loving you
has become as natural
to me as breathing.
And know also that,
as I quietly thank God
each day for my life . . .
in the same whisper,
I thank Him for you.

— S. M. Beard

There was a time when I thought
that I could never share my life
    with another.
I thought I was too much of
    an individual;
I didn't want to give up any part
    of me for anyone else.
I didn't want to make sacrifices.

But then, you came into my life,
and my whole attitude changed.
I learned that with you,
I don't have to give up
    any part of me.
You make me better.
With you, I don't mind compromising,
    making sacrifices,
even giving in . . .
    because I love you.

— Karla J. Manarchy

Wherever you are
there is the sparkle of sunlight
From your soul
I draw the presence of peace
Love's praise surrounds you
in silence and in song
I love you season by season
by day and by night
with all of my life.

— Dorie Runyon

There are so many things
that I've never said to you —
things that I've never been able to say
    or never had the perfect opportunity . . .
but I've always wanted you to know that
you've given my life so much . . .

There are times when you've trusted me
    and been forgiving, understanding,
there are times, so many times,
when you made me feel
that I was worth something as a person . . .

You deserve so much thanks,
but it's really not the kind
        that I can repay —
you've done so much already in life,
I don't know that I could add to
the wealth of love and compassion
        that you already hold.

But I do know that
if there's anything
that I can *ever* do for you —
        all you have to do is ask,
and I'll try my best
        and I'll give my best
and I'll always want the best . . . for you.

— Andrew Tawney

You may think that
I haven't noticed all of
the thoughtful little things
    you do for me . . .
I know that I don't always
    say "thanks" . . .
But I have noticed,
and it's all those
    little things
and more . . .
that make me love you
    the way I do.

— amanda pierce

I can remember the first time
    I saw you
and how I knew that I wanted
to get to know you better . . .
To see in your eyes the little
things that made you happy
was like seeing a rainbow
or a butterfly dancing
or walking in the rain
Getting to know . . .
    the bigger things
like caring, understanding
and love
Getting to know . . .
the extraordinary depth of
    your mind,
the power of your love
Getting to know you better . . .
I hope it never ends.

— Jeanne Marie Cooney

Love . . .
all of my life
I have
read of it
dreamed of it
waited for it
cried alone for it
searched for it
needed it.
Now, in you,
I have found it.

— Sandee Ahmann

When I look at you,
I see all of the people
  that I've ever loved;
all of the dreams
  that I've ever had;
all of the wishes
  that I've ever spoken;
And
all of the hopes
  that I have for tomorrow.

— Martin A. Arce

In my mind, I liken our relationship
to that of a brilliant sunrise.
In the beginning
our love was breathtakingly beautiful,
full of fire and passion.
And as the sun began to rise
    on the horizon
the passion did not die,
    nor the fire go out,
but the relationship took on a
    different — more permanent hue.
The feelings, though never completely
    void of self-centeredness,
began to focus on the other person's
    needs, wants and desires.
The incredible emotion of new love
    was replaced
with a softer concern, caring
    and love for the other person . . .

The focus became the need
    of just being together —
to be a support in time of sorrow
    and pain,
to help the other person grow
    as an individual,
to trust the other person completely,
to love with openness and honesty,
to give as well as receive,
to talk with frankness about any
    and all problems,
to be a best friend,
to love and be loved — now.

In our relationship,
    as in a sunrise,
the sun is our love
that lights the path of life
and that is felt so deeply
    in our souls.

— Thomas R. Dudley

I try sometimes
to imagine us
together when we are older,
and it seems to me . . .

that I shall
only love you
        more.

— Gustave Flaubert

Let us take this moment to remember
the joy, the beauty and the love
that we have shared in our lives
together.

Let us take this moment to remember
all the special moments
that have weaved their way into
our hearts, bringing us closer
together.

Let us take this moment to remember
the fulfillment, the contentment
and the many moments to come
in our beautiful, loving life
together.

— David P. Jacobs

We have the ability
    and opportunity
to build the type of
    relationship
known by so very few
And in my heart, my mind
    and my deepest soul,
I think it will come to be
because it feels so very
    right and natural
to grow and become closer
    to you.

— Johnnie Rosenauer

I never imagined
anyone like you in my life
but now that I know
of the wonders and feelings
that you bring,
I could never imagine
my life
being without you.

— jonivan

As I dream my dreams
   of how life should be,
you are always there . . .
to share in my laughter,
   my joys and tears,
to comfort my sorrows
   and calm my fears
We're always together —
   hand in hand —
living the dreams
   we both have planned
loving each other
   wherever we go . . .
I know I'll continue
   to dream my dreams
always living each one
   through
together with you
forever in love . . .
         just me and you.

— Debbie Avery

I love you.
I am telling you now,
so that you never need to wonder
　　　or to feel unsure.
If I wait for the perfect moment
　　　to tell you . . .
　　　it may never come.
And if I just assume that you know,
　　　you may never be certain.
So I am telling you now,
　　　and I shall tell you
　　　many times again . . .
　　　that I love you.

— Sue Mitchell

Please . . . listen closely,
for I have something
   to whisper to you
that my spoken words
         can't quite express.
I've heard it said that
the meanings that come from
   hearts and smiles
      and touches and tears
aren't nearly as stubborn as words;
and I know now that it's true . . .

for when you make me smile
   so bright that I feel like
      glowing inside;

or you touch me so exquisitely
   that I know our love
      really does have magic . . .

or you do something so sweet
 that it overwhelms me to think
  that someone as wonderful as you
  could care so much for me . . .

It's then that the feelings
 in my heart
  say such wonderful words.
I wish you could hear them
 the way I do . . . because they say
  so many beautiful things to you.

       — Andrew Tawney

Love is . . .
    patient
    forgiving
    caring
    undemanding
    and loyal
I hope that you know
how much it means to me
to fulfill
these feelings
in my love
for you.

— Beth Lee

Since I began to care for you,
I have reached heights
and touched depths
I never dreamed of before.

— Ellen Thorney-Croft Fowler

I am always here
to understand you
I am always here
to laugh with you
I am always here
to cry with you
I am always here
to talk with you
I am always here
to think with you
I am always here
to plan with you
Even though we
might not always
be together
please know that
I am always
here to
love
you

— Susan Polis Schutz

I more than love you . . .
I trust you,
I believe in you.
I give to you my life,
my dreams,
And all of my tomorrows.
I care about you
with all my heart.
Beyond every creed that
I believe . . .
I more than love you.

— Shalynn Gillespie

You, Wonderful You

I love being with you —
    I really do;
I don't think I've ever known
    anyone in my life that
    I felt as easy
    to be with . . . as you.
You can make me laugh and smile
    and just feel nice;
    just feel good about being alive . . .

I'm not sure
    what I want to say to you
    for all you do . . .
Maybe "thanks" for adding
    so much to my days;
Maybe "it really means a lot"
    to have you as a part of my life —
    to have a special sharing
    that I hope will last
        my whole life through;
And maybe . . . "please . . ."
    please let me know
        if there's anything
            I can ever
                do for you.

— Laine Parsons

It is my greatest wish
to give you all the love
you could ever need
To touch you
so that you will know
that I am always there
To cherish you
above all others
To respect you
and to remind you
that you are
the one
I love.

— jonivan

Let's never stop making
   memories
for the ones we have
    are so good
They're something I've come
    to depend upon
in times when I need a lift
On dark days, lonely days,
   quiet days
    and happy days,
you're never too far
    from my heart
And of all the days still ahead,
   you'll always be a special
   part.

— amanda pierce

There will never be . . .

There will never be a day
when I won't smile a quiet smile
and say an unspoken thanks . . .
            just for you.

There will never come a time
when I won't think of
all the special things about you —
      you with the gentle touch
      and the warming grin
      and the kindest eyes
            I've ever known.

It makes such a difference
to have someone like you
to go through life with;
I've discovered that I need
the kind of sharing that we have;
and I want the kind of feelings
      that we share
            to continue day into day
                  into all of our tomorrows . . .

For there will never be
            a day in my life
                  that you will not be a part of.

— Laine Parsons

I wanted you to know today
that you are especially on my mind
and in my prayers.
You are such a beautiful, loving person.
You give so much of yourself to others.
I pray that God's many blessings
will be yours — today and every day.
You are a blessing
            to so many, and
I love you very much.

— Jan Kirkley Boyd

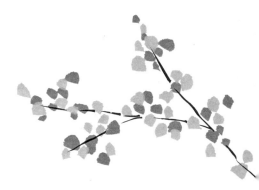

ACKNOWLEDGMENTS

We gratefully acknowledge the permission granted by the following authors, publishers and authors' representatives to reprint poems and excerpts from their publications.

Barbara A. Billings for "If I could give you," by Barbara A. Billings. Copyright © Barbara A. Billings, 1983. All rights reserved. Reprinted by permission.

Johnnie Rosenauer for "I have given a lot of thought" and for "We have the ability," by Johnnie Rosenauer. Copyright © Johnnie Rosenauer, 1983. All rights reserved. Reprinted by permission.

Laura West for "i wish for you warmth," by Laura West. Copyright © Laura West, 1982. All rights reserved. Reprinted by permission.

Genevieve Bartels Wichmann for "Did you know . . . ," by Genevieve Bartels Wichmann . Copyright © Genevieve Bartels Wichmann, 1983. All rights reserved. Reprinted by permission.

Rowland R. Hoskins, Jr. for "Once when I was younger," by Rowland R. Hoskins, Jr. Copyright © Rowland R. Hoskins, Jr., 1983. All rights reserved. Reprinted by permission.

Marci Dee Lowinger for "Our relationship," by Marci Dee Lowinger. Copyright © Marci Dee Lowinger, 1983. All rights reserved. Reprinted by permission.

Diane Westlake for "constant companion," by Diane Westlake. Copyright © Diane Westlake, 1980. All rights reserved. Reprinted by permission.

Colleen Williams for "As each day goes by," by Colleen Williams. Copyright © Colleen Williams, 1983. All rights reserved. Reprinted by permission.

S. M. Beard for "If at times you think," by S. M. Beard. Copyright © S. M. Beard, 1983. All rights reserved. Reprinted by permission.

Karla J. Manarchy for "There was a time," by Karla J. Manarchy. Copyright © Karla J. Manarchy, 1983. All rights reserved. Reprinted by permission.

Dorie Runyon for "Wherever you are," by Dorie Runyon. Copyright © Dorie Runyon, 1983. All rights reserved. Reprinted by permission.

Jeanne Marie Cooney for "I can remember the first time," by Jeanne Marie Cooney. Copyright © Jeanne Marie Cooney, 1983. All rights reserved. Reprinted by permission.

Sandee Ahmann for "Love . . . ," by Sandee Ahmann. Copyright © Sandee Ahmann, 1983. All rights reserved. Reprinted by permission.

Martin A. Arce for "When I look at you," by Martin A. Arce. Copyright © Martin A. Arce, 1983. All rights reserved. Reprinted by permission.

Thomas R. Dudley for "In my mind," by Thomas R. Dudley. Copyright © Thomas R. Dudley, 1983. All rights reserved. Reprinted by permission.

David P. Jacobs for "Let us take this moment to remember," by David P. Jacobs. Copyright © David P. Jacobs, 1983. All rights reserved. Reprinted by permission.

jonivan for "I never imagined," by jonivan. Copyright © jonivan, 1983. And for "It is my greatest wish," by jonivan. Copyright © jonivan, 1982. All rights reserved. Reprinted by permission.

Debbie Avery for "As I dream my dreams," by Debbie Avery. Copyright © Debbie Avery, 1983. All rights reserved. Reprinted by permission.

Sue Mitchell for "I love you," by Sue Mitchell. Copyright © Sue Mitchell, 1982. All rights reserved. Reprinted by permission.

Jan Kirkley Boyd for "I wanted you to know today," by Jan Kirkley Boyd. Copyright © Jan Kirkley Boyd, 1982. All rights reserved. Reprinted by permission.

Shalynn Gillespie for "I more than love you . . . ," by Shalynn Gillespie. Copyright © Shalynn Gillespie, 1983. All rights reserved. Reprinted by permission.

A careful effort has been made to trace the ownership of poems used in this anthology in order to obtain permission to reprint copyrighted material and to give proper credit to the copyright owners.

If any error or omission has occurred, it is completely inadvertent, and we would like to make corrections in future editions provided that written notification is made to the publisher: BLUE MOUNTAIN PRESS, INC., P.O. Box 4549, Boulder, Colorado 80306.